What I Love about

____

1

I love your

____.

2

You are my favorite

____

in the world.

3

I love hearing stories
about your

____.

4

I love how talented
you are at

____.

5

When we are apart,
it makes me happy to think about

________________________________.

6

I believe we'd make a great

____

team.

7

I love to watch you

______________________________________.

8

You deserve the

____

award.

9

I love the sound of your

____

when you

______________________________.

10

If you were a holiday,
you'd be

______________________________.

11

It's hard to put into words how strongly I feel about your

____.

12

I love how good you are
at giving me

______________________________.

13

I wish I had known you when

____.

14

I love how you make

____.

15

I love going to

____

with you.

16

I love to kiss your

__________________________________.

17

You have the greatest taste in

________________________________.

18

I love how you

____

every day.

19

If you wanted to, you could easily

______________________________________.

20

You make me want to be a better

______________________________.

21

I would love to create a

____

for you.

22

I love to play

____

with you.

23

I believe the world needs your unique

______________________________________.

24

I am so glad that you love my

____.

25

We should totally

____

together.

26

I love how you want to

______________________________________.

27

If you were a color, you'd be

____.

28

I still can't believe you

____.

29

I love how you

____

my

____.

30

It is so incredibly funny when you

____.

31

I love how you have such strong

______________________________________.

32

You give the best

____.

33

I love remembering the time we

____.

34

I love to

____

your

_______________________________________.

35

Everyone should be as

____

as you.

36

I love it when you

____

like

____.

37

I never get tired of your

______________________________.

38

I love how you never get tired of my

____.

39

I love to

____

for you.

40

I love the feel of your

____.

41

I'd like to take you to

______________________________.

42

I love it when you wear

____.

43

If you were a dessert, you'd be

______________________________.

44

I always want to hear what you're going to say about

____.

45

I love how you love

____.

46

I love how you believe in

____.

47

I am kind of obsessed
with your

____.

48

I love how you

me.

49

Nobody else can

____

like you.

50

I am so

____

that

______________________________________.

I Love You.

Created and published by Knock Knock
Distributed by Who's There Inc.
Venice, CA 90291
knockknockstuff.com

Made in China

ISBN: 978-160106493-6 **UPC**: 825703-50061-5

14 15